DEGREES OF LATITUDE

For Susan & Linelle —
with pleasure & best wishes —
Laurel.

Also by Laurel Blossom

Wednesday: New and Selected Poems (2004)

The Papers Said (1993)

What's Wrong (1987)

Any Minute (chapbook) (1979)

as editor

Lovely Village of the Hills: Twentieth Century Edgefield Poetry (2007)

Splash! Great Writing about Swimming (1997)

Many Lights in Many Windows: Twenty Years of Great Poetry and Fiction from The Writers Community (1996)

Oxygen: Poems of Beatrice Danziger (1988)

DEGREES OF LATITUDE

a poem by

Laurel Blossom (signature)

Laurel Blossom

Four Way Books
Tribeca / New York City

Distributed by
University Press of New England
Hanover and London

Editorial Office
Four Way Books
POB 535, Village Station
New York, NY 10014
www.fourwaybooks.com

Library of Congress Cataloging-in-Publication Data

Blossom, Laurel.
Degrees of latitude : a poem / by Laurel Blossom.
    p. cm.
ISBN-13: 978-1-884800-80-1 (pbk. : acid-free paper)
ISBN-10: 1-884800-80-7 (pbk. : acid-free paper)
I. Title.
PS3552.L677D44 2007
811'.54--dc22
2007019421

Cover design: K.C. Witherell / Hello Studio.

This book is manufactured in the United States of America. Four Way Books
is a not-for-profit literary press. We are grateful for the assistance we receive
from individual donors, public arts agencies, and private foundations.

This publication is made possible with public funds from
the New York State Council on the Arts, a state agency.

Distributed by University Press of New England
One Court Street, Lebanon, NH 03766

[clmp]
We are a proud member of the Council of Literary Magazines and Presses.

To Ken

Contents

...representation of space was malleable...

...Nor was time fixed...

...the past was always present...

Peter Whitfield
The Image of the World

THE NORTH POLE

At sea: midsummer midnight. Night as (light as) day.

Ice so blue it's frozen sky lit from within, above, below.

In my cabin, pictures of my son and me in Nairobi, me and my father at the North Cape, Lionel at home in New York City.

On the ship's P.A., Belafonte singing *Day-O*.

Ivory gulls, like memory, at the edge of vision.

My mother on the green green lawn, laughing up at me laughing, drying my eyes.

Following channels through the ice (the mind) called leads.

Awakened by a great crash of ice against the hull.

Pitching and rolling as if through water, grinding as if through rock.

Our homely Russian nuclear icebreaker, crazy red dot on a flat blank map.

I thought you were opposed to nuclear power, said Will.

On the bridge, the Captain watches the ship shove up, over one last pressure ridge.

89° 59. 993.

We know from a satellite radio beam, like a finger of light: YOU ARE HERE.

Overture to *Götterdämmerung*.

We are one hundred warm-blooded human creatures.

In our red down jackets eating hamburgers rare and french fries iced with tomato ketchup.

Taking each other's living pictures by a flagpole on a shroud of moving ice.

Armed guards walking the invisible perimeter, Rod Stewart crooning to the bent horizon.

Polar bears sniff the vast, reverberated air.

And the Captain says he came up out of the swimming hole wanting to shout for joy, but couldn't.

The cold had taken his breath away.

Trap door, coffin lid, going under thrill.

I came up wanting to shout: *Get me out of here!*

Five kilometers deep, 3°(F) below freezing.

Cold as childhood.

Ladies and gents, I did shout it!

THE ARCTIC CIRCLE

We all lived together in the big stone house, my mother, my father, my two brothers and me.

Like bats, avoiding each other by radar.

o

Even now:

When we (that is, Lionel and I) invite Buddy and his wife to go dancing, he says there's a thirty percent chance.

No, he says, *you have to understand. That's up from zero.*

o

Thirty-five million years ago. Ice began to form.

o

In my crib I could hear them by the fireless fireside.

In silhouette, silent, my Arctic family circle: mother, father, Buddy, Will.

My father might have called it a *den of inequity.*

In the dark above my crib: spirals swirling.

In my held breath: *Aurora borealis.*

o

The dresser drawer full of grosgrain ribbons, all the colors.

Our two faces in the icy looking glass.

As she braided my bright hair together each morning and tied the lovely ribbons tight.

o

But like iron shavings to a magnet, all the cells of my braided body lined up looking at her, compass-spinning turn of her head, her fingers pushing a filter cigarette into its Dunhill filter holder. She was my Farthest North, magnetic pole.

I knew all about her, I knew everything there was.

How to tell Hepplewhite, how to wash kid gloves.

How to walk home with my school books on my head, fluted Ionic column.

o

Even though at night things changed shape without warning, white glare beneath my bedroom door, mumbling loud a long way off.

Something tears (as if now), something hard (a head) hits a floor,

10

something (perhaps a father) falls on top of something (mother, maybe).

Deep in that frozen wilderness, three A.M.

Darkness like a mouth, stopped. Door like a stone.

o

Later we (that is, my mother and I) lived in a basement apartment, already half underground.

The slick Hungarian garage mechanic on the other side of the steel fire door.

Convinced he was going to rape her.

Her or me. *It's the same,* she said, *thing.*

o

Every night out the window she watched the red-rimmed sun go down.

Beyond the street that used to be a river.

Below the waterline.

I picked up her fear, her longing like infection, her liquid cure.

o

On the other hand:

Sitting in the casement window in a suite at the Biltmore Hotel.

My adolescent arms around my adolescent knees.

Syncopated lights, neon horns. New York City.

Mother, I said, I'm home.

I still wake up, stop in the middle, I can't believe I'm here: Pinch me!

At the Palm Court, she ordered a frozen daiquiri.

A few minutes later: *Certainly, madam.* This one she gave to me.

In French, she said, *the word is debonair. The debonair shall inherit the earth.*

Nobody ever had such a beautiful mother.

o

One of us (in front of her fireplace) would call the other (in front of hers): *Have you got your wine? Have you got your cigarettes?*

o

My mother said, *Women who feel empty may think they want a baby.*

I thought I wanted a cigarette, a chocolate milkshake, I thought I wanted a Scotch on the rocks.

My mother said, *Your husband will leave you if you can't slice carrots.*

My mother said, *Honey, I think you're pregnant.*

Mother, I said, the entire cruise ship is seasick except you. Including the crew.

Nevertheless, my mother said.

o

This is a picture of me and my mother standing in the square outside our hotel in Athens.

This is a picture of me and my mother and my son who isn't born yet standing in the square outside in Athens.

This is a picture of me and my mother who isn't dead yet and my son who isn't born yet standing in the square outside.

o

Metastasis: beginning of loss and longing.

o

The baby cried in the middle of the night, he wasn't hungry, his diapers were dry, he wouldn't burp.

13

What was I doing in here all alone in the middle of the night with a newborn baby.

I'll give you something to cry about, I told him.

When I spanked him, when he cried so hard he gulped, when I knew why.

I held him close, rocked him until he slept, sang lullabies.

Across the degrees, across the separation.

The sound of him, fact of his actual breathing, my Harry.

o

If I recognize him now in the sea of mortarboards, how he raises his sunglasses to his head.

If I try to drive my flag into the axis, heart, the utmost, ninetieth degree of him: *mine*.

If I come that close.

Within what my father might have called *a hair's breath*.

But don't.

If I let him be: fragile, beloved, uninhabitable.

We cannot belong to the ends of the earth.

o

Around her kitchen table my mother arranged a set of ladder-back chairs, painted on the backs with the names of her grandchildren.

Christopher Robert Stephanie Barbara Harrison Jane

Rounded top rungs like bite-sized tombstones.

o

Last night I almost took a bottle of sleeping pills.

Mother, I think you should see a psychiatrist.

I wish you'd told me that six months ago when I really needed one.

o

Then Buddy tried to pry the lid off barehanded.

Proceedings (funereal) interrupted: screwdriver, can opener.

When we resumed, down by the river:

The Lord is my shepherd, I lift up mine eyes, Our Father, Make me an instrument.

Will lifted the lid, turned the box upside down. Up swarmed her ashes into our faces, like bees.

Fall gently into the waters they did not.

They were not docile, no, neither were they dead.

Harry tried to catch them, Harry waved his little hand, *good-bye*.

○

My uncle came back with me for one last nightcap.

How pretty you look, just like your mother.

As I sat in her green leather chair beneath the heather blue painting.

My mother's brother making a pass at me in the buried apartment.

Both of us drunk on the day of her goddamn funeral.

○

Arms out, fingers scratching, wind whipping her dead white hair, *good-bye* again.

She likes to practice this over and over.

You don't know that for a fact, says Harry. *You don't know your mother killed herself.*

The rigid, frigid, livid, and beloved.

o

Self-portrait in red and white striped T-shirt. Pigtails yellow with red ribbons and, even though the paper is white, white stripes in white crayon to make them still whiter.

As if that could stop her.

As if our two faces were one in the looking glass.

o

Projection of a three-dimensional sphere onto a two-dimensional plane.

Impossible, says Harry, *without distortion.*

Harry, earth scientist. Lover of maps.

o

I want my mommy.

I hear her say, *I* am *your mommy.*

Nevertheless.

THE TEMPERATE ZONE

Anywhere, she told him, *even Hudson, Ohio.*

She wrote from the hospital. The doctors called it *separation anxiety.*

She'd had her nails painted, she was startled every time she saw her own hands, they didn't look real.

If that's what you want, even that, she would, she was going to be so glad to see him, she called him *angel.*

She said she'd live on a farm to make him happy. She'd be the best damn hostess in the county. She'd make it the prettiest damn farm.

Everything was going to be fine when the war was over.

She was never going to have another nervous breakdown.

o

He sent her a pocketbook from Berlin. She thought it was meant for his mother or his sister Phoebe.

Everything I send you is for you unless you choose to give it away.

o

She served wine with dinner. *Two nights in a row,* she wrote him.

It tastes better than milk and it's easier than iced tea.

o

21

Dressed in her Scotch plaid suit, lines of yellow, red, green on a navy field.

Here she is.

She looks the way she must have looked the day he fell in love with her.

The day I fall in love with her, I'm not as tall as she is and I want to be a boy, except when I look at her, I want to be like her.

Not like her. I want to be her and him looking at her.

o

He touches her small breasts that are like my small breasts.

She touches his big swimmer's shoulders that are like my big swimmer's shoulders.

They rock back and forth, they kiss with their mouths like my mouth, open, they close as I close my eyes their eyes.

She touches his skin as smooth as my own.

The hair between our legs is the same, she spreads her legs lovely he runs his hands over as I run mine over mine as he enters, as they were then, as I imagine them.

o

A picture of the couple in happier times.

o

She made herself into the best damn hostess.

She made it the prettiest damn farm.

Then he sent her a postcard from his mother's in Palm Beach.

Everything I do, it read, *is for you. Everything I've done for fifteen years.*

Everything they told themselves was a lie.

o

Come home, she wrote him, *your children miss you.*

Come home, now that your blood pressure's down.

Come home, your problems are purely emotional.

Come home, angel, come home.

Everything they told each other was a trap.

o

Can't you remember to wipe your shoes? she said. Her high heels *tsked* across the tile.

The terrible mouth opened up inside her, spewed its black smoke into the ordinary air.

You should have seen him buckle and cave. His body shifted on its ivory girders.

Teetered, stood. He had been almost smiling.

The uninvited cold had come in with him.

His rubbers were covered with snow, he took his hat off, he stood dripping, *plick, plick,* on the vestibule floor.

She stood like Cerberus, five foot four.

o

They called us onto the porch to tell us.

She sat on the couch, he sank in a chair. *Do you have any questions?*

We had none, we had thousands, we had one. *You may go now.*

o

My brothers to their Rorschach rooms, lying on their plaid and tufted bedspreads with their hands behind their heads, doors open, staring at their separate ceilings.

They said nothing to each other. Will was crying, Buddy was not.

o

I was on my bike riding out to the meadow, lying on the grass with my hands behind my head, staring at the sky as if it were a ceiling.

I was like Will, I was crying. I was like Buddy, I was not.

o

Daddy called it a *legal separation*.

I thought it was one of his malaprops. It was not.

A legal separation. As opposed to what?

Though I was in the next room, I said nothing.

White (why) space.

o

How every name implies its absence.

o

Daddy standing in the driveway, gone.

Staring straight ahead. Not at me. But like me.

Growing smaller.

Smaller.

As we each disappeared. Into the minutes, into the degrees.

o

Homeless (homesick) at the horizon.

Homeless (homesick) at the core.

o

My hair is dirty, I haven't washed it since Monday, it stays where you put it.

Makes you want people not to see you. You pin it under a hat or up, it doesn't look so dirty up.

Maybe you cut it short, and what if you don't have a hat in this weather.

You have to sleep on a bench, a snow bank, an empty stomach.

I'm dressed in layers, it's the style.

I used to be pretty, I used to be rich, I used to have my nails done every single week and sometimes, even then, I didn't take a shower.

I used to give people a quarter if they asked me nicely. If they made a joke.

I stand back, I can't smell myself myself. The cold has its good points, sweat freezes, odors pinch off like buds.

o

I'm wearing this new pair of shoes at Soup Kitchen.

Mary Jane says how much she likes them.

Mary Jane says how much she likes them, she's seen a similar pair at Lord & Taylor.

She says she's thinking of buying them, what do I think?

Don't, because this pair of shoes slides off the heel, makes my toes itch.

Too bad, she says, *they sure are pretty.*

They sure are pretty, says the next guy in line. *Where'd you get them?*

I don't remember.

Take one off, he says, *maybe it says.*

I take one off. It says.

You have a nice arch.

No, I don't. I have no arch at all. My feet are flat.

Oh no. Put your foot down, spread your toes. It's okay, really, I studied podiatry in college. Spread your toes, lift your heel.

What's he doing, says Mary Jane.

Examining my foot.

She has very pretty feet. He bends down. He starts massaging the arch.

Please get up.

He looks at me. *You have very pretty feet.*

I say thank you.

o

I went to college in New York because the drinking age was eighteen.

That's how I got here in the first place.

o

My father's new wife wore wedgies and ankle socks.

My mother shriveled and died. It was the nerves.

My father exploded on the golf course. It was the heart.

My father's new wife became my father's new widow.

o

Either they weren't happy and they thought they were or they weren't happy and they knew it or they were happy and they thought they weren't or they were happy and they knew it.

And that's what killed them.

o

My advice? said Aunt Phoebe. *Take out the becauses.*

o

My friend Gloria says, *A man on the bus shoved his face in my face. If you want pussy, he said, you should go to Greenwich Village.*

We were at a coffee shop, swapping New York stories.

o

I was hit by a messenger on a bike, says Frank, *thrown a full parking space, knocked out. We collided head to head.*

When I woke up I didn't know. It sounded like a bomb had gone off in my brain.

My doctor told me I shouldn't have taken that aspirin, I shouldn't have gone to bed.

You have to keep moving.

o

Annabelle says, *When he got near me, he threw out his arm, it hit me in the head, a woman caught me from behind.*

Are you all right, she said, what happened, who was that, do you know him?

o

Judy says, *I was sitting on the subway when a man and his wife came and stood in front of me, well-dressed, respectable.*

He said I was in his seat and punched me in the face.

o

I was hailing a cab, says Peter. *A car went by with the window down. I was hit in the stomach by two eggs.*

Hard. Hard-boiled.

o

Two more children killed by stray bullets.

Harry's best friend mugged on 59th St.

Tourist knifed by seven teens for money to go dancing at Roseland.

Lionel threatened on the subway platform.

Housewife washing dishes at her kitchen sink.

Four-year-old playing in a Brooklyn playground.

Bullets flying thick as pigeons. Bullets through the glass alas.

o

Where are you going when you go? asks Nancy.

Forty-room houses in Cleveland Heights are going for 85 grand, says Frank.

Exxon's moving to Texas, says Peter.

I'm going to Portland, to chiropractic, says Mary Jane.

We were *thinking of San Francisco,* says Gloria.

Until the quake.

o

Then we fly in from somewhere else, rivers like mercury or (see) streaks of gold, Manhattan's own very specific gravity.

I turn to Harry: Forget it.

I turn to Lionel: Forget it, forget somewhere (anywhere) else.

o

A my-age woman passes me in Macintosh, sisal bag, rain boots, corduroys. Make-up: none. Curly yellow hair shoulder-length and flying.

Intellectual, academic, feminist, deep.

Excuse me, I say in my red language.

I'm in my silk jacquard dress, sheer stockings, heels, hair coiffed, red lipstick extending outside the lip line, eye shadow: Please!

I only *look* superficial, mascara that runs when I cry.

I love that.

o

The temperate zone is where it rains some and it snows some and the sun shines some, it is not extreme.

No, neither is it docile.

But it changeth as the seasons and the cycle of the sun.

o

He says he's the grandson of Mellon.

Carnegie Mellon? the bag lady asks.

They're sitting across from me, Penn Station.

Yeah, he says, *big estate. I had to go out there. It was my birthday.*

He crosses one homeless leg over the other, creases his pant leg with scissor fingers.

32

They spent 80 grand on my party.

She whistles.

o

Can you spare $500? asks the beggar.

OK, then, how 'bout a quarter.

o

The bag lady points to her wriggling toes.

If boots are a problem, she laughs, *borrow mine.*

o

So the social worker asked me this stupid question. She said where do you want to live?

So I said I'll take Sutton Place.

o

Shivering outside St. Ignatius Loyola, penis the color of his colorless clothes.

Peeing politely in a puddle of drain water.

o

Don't, says the beggar, imitating the social worker. *Don't give them money on the street, it just encourages them.*

o

The bag lady says, *I could tell it was Van Johnson because they were talking deals.*

So I said to the cashier, I said, isn't that Van Johnson?

She just looked at me, so I said: I used to be a celebrity. I used to be pretty. I used to be rich.

o

It was Good Friday.

We were serving our usual eight tables of eight.

Somebody noticed one of the tables missing four sandwiches and pieces of cake.

But the volunteer remembered distinctly: full tray, how she placed them at each.

Finally the crew chief halved some cakes, quartered sandwiches.

Our clients took their sixty-four places.

Later four new people showed up. We made room for them under the Sunday nametags.

Silverware, coffee, soup when one of them pointed at the piano.

Out of the minutes, out of the degrees.

Four sandwiches, four pieces of cake through the glare. We saw them appear, we watched them decide.

o

Is the forsythia more golden, more bursting this year, or is it just me?

Sprigs of yellow splashing like lit-up ocean spray.

Shadows of branches on white brick façades.

How the rules happen to be these and not others.

Trees bare in winter to let the pale sun through.

Summer shade. Scarf of sunlight fluttering.

White fence's glare against a graphite sky.

I love that.

o

I took the baby to Palm Beach to meet my father's mother. By then, she didn't really know who I was exactly.

You know, she said, *I never much liked my son's first wife.*

(That is, my mother.)

                        °

You have to keep moving.

TROPICS N

Just barely, I tell Will. Sub-tropics.

He spends the winter in a white stucco house by a mangrove swamp where it hardly ever rains.

My little cracker house in a sea oaks grove five miles up the road, five degrees cooler.

Rains here every afternoon.

I love that.

o

My father wrote the General:

In fact I have been in Berlin three months, and in these three months I have had no job that would occupy one full day's work.

I suppose I will have to wait until others of longer service here are returned.

Meantime, perhaps you will give me the encouragement of your counsel, and even—somehow, sometime—help me to get home.

He told the General how much he missed his family.

Named names, Buddy, Will, me.

o

Meantime, my mother ate the vermouth-soaked olives.

She wore print dresses with square necklines, short-capped sleeves, pearl chokers, red lipstick, hair pulled back in what was called a *snood*.

The army wives. They leaned across tables, intimate in conversation.

Red-tipped cigarettes extended, flattering their lovely hands, their lifted chins.

When their friends called martinis an *acquired taste*, they acquired it.

The home front, said my mother, *was so damn much fun.*

Rations, said Aunt Phoebe, *blackouts, women and kids. The home front was so damn much trouble.*

o

Homeless (homesick) on the home front.

Sick of my homeless home.

o

I can still smell the starched, pink polished cotton.

Heady, sweet swoon of orange blossoms.

Phoebe took our picture. I was in mary janes and ankle socks. Pigtails with fat pink grosgrain ribbons.

His mother waited lunch.

We sat on the west porch looking at the lake.

My brothers got to go outside to play pirates.

The women smoothed their minute-hand watches. They ticked and ticked.

By the time he arrived, my mother was blaming the war on him.

Welcome home, welcome home. *Daddy, angel, Daddy!*

o

In some places, Harry tells me, *only six miles down, the molten hot stuff, the magma.*

o

Also if they're tied to their mothers they can't object if you're tied to yours.

They keep the same distance.

Will I ever be interested in a man who's not a Mama's boy?

o

It's enough just to love a place, says Will, *you don't necessarily have to know why.*

o

In from the ocean late afternoon, hot skin, cool tiles, dark interiors.

Water ran from the large-mouthed faucets, tub so big in my grandmother's big, shingled house by the saltwater-smelling sea.

We floated.

Sand clung to the skin, chips of mica, sand in the hair, in the nose, in the armpits, belly button, folds of the penis, vagina, sand in the ears, under nails, in eyelashes.

Spray-crusted, sea-dunked, sun-crisp, happy as celery.

o

We always knew where we were. In the middle, in the (humid) muddle, in the more or less.

Sun up through the east door facing the ocean, last rays through the lakeside porch's screen.

Hallway (halfway) where morning and evening met.

Light pouring in, pouring out, side to side through my father's mariachi martini cocktail shaker.

Swizzle stick, newel post, axis of all that mattered.

o

One day my grandmother took me to the unused corner room.

She showed me the cupboards, broken shells and halves of buttons, shredded costumes, crumpled shoes, fishing and butterfly nets, golden books.

The mildewy smell of not having been opened since.

Everything dark and sweet with unknowing.

She left me there but it was not alone.

The world inside the world, the secret entrance.

o

Looked like a black garden hose snaking across.

As I walked to the saltwater pool in the morning through the steamy jungle alone in my girlhood.

Sliding as if some thicketed gardener pulled a hose behind him to water the dark.

Tropical smell of sweetness and decay.

o

Sat, the two of us, Daddy and me, in the cool dark room while the sunshine blazed like blazes.

Whose idea was it, was it his, this you and me, did I cry, did I tell him how much I missed him, forgive him for going into that place called *overseas*.

Did he promise never again to leave me, so that later I rode out to the meadow, green desert, lay down betrayed beneath the hot blue sky.

o

But before that.

In the all-alone night I set fire to the bedclothes.

I made stink bombs and cow pies, I made my brothers drink green milk, eat rhubarb, I made them jump from a ten-foot high wall into five feet of mud, into quicksand, *duck soup.*

I made Buddy kiss me on the mouth.

I made Will dye his hair blue.

I blew down their trestle of cards that curved from the top of the spiral stairs through all the bedrooms but mine, I refused to let them.

It was longer than anybody could have built except my two brothers.

I bet you're sorry, they said.

Am not.

o

When I tied people up, I beat them to a pulp. They all turned out to have blue hair and dimples.

I learned to close only one eye the way Will could. I learned after months of holding my right eyebrow down, to lift the left one only, so it would arch.

Will you please tell my sister, said Buddy to my mother, *to stop wearing my basey cap.*

o

They tied me up, killed my father the rancher, rode off into the sunset, some other map, the unknown, the glare.

Leaving me at the cabin door. They said, *You're a good crier.*

o

Will fell off his bike, I ran to help.

Later he said it wasn't *that* he was hurt so much as *where*.

All I wanted to do was: Let me see.

Buddy asked me to show him my breasts.

I pulled down the straps of my new two-piece bathing suit.

He looked, he said nothing, he swam away.

o

Try it, two for two dollars, nothing ventured, called the barker.

First ball went in, *piece o' cake*, but I missed the second.

Rim shot, he explained.

Then he demonstrated. *Here*, he said, *try again*.

This time my ball stayed in, on top of his. He took them both out.

Tell you what.

He said he'd give me the flamingo free if I could get just one ball in, *that's it*.

But the price went up to five bucks.

One did go in.

Rim shot, he said, shaking his head, *take it over*.

You know how I let you take the rim shot over when it bounced back out, well, I'm going to let you take this one over too.

Suddenly, he reminded me of my two brothers.

That I wasn't going to win that stupid flamingo.

○

Oh, sunshine hot as a man's big hands (I thought).

Oh, air slow with orange blossoms and sweat!

o

The paper's not white, what it says doesn't have to be spotless.

This truth holds also for tablecloths.

o

When I answered the phone.

When I heard a stranger's voice.

When he told me he was going to make me feel good.

When he told me to lie down.

When I was curious, when I was young.

When he said to unbutton my blouse, slowly.

Slip the bra strap off my shoulder.

Slide my hand to my breast. Push the bra down below.

Touch the nipples, put the phone down, pinch.

Hello! Hello! When he said could I hear him.

Move your hands over your stomach, press down.

Raise your knees.

Put one finger in. Now two, three, your fist, the phone receiver.

o

My little cracker house in a sea oaks grove.

Reminds my brothers of my grandmother's house.

It creaks, says Buddy. *Smells of mildew*, says Will.

Air humid as a (secret) hug.

o

Then I was sitting on my mother's belly on the green green grass in the tropical sunshine.

The crabgrass bounced.

She looked so pretty, sun shining, Daddy home from that dreadful war.

She must have said something so funny, something about my stupid brothers.

I had to, even though I didn't want to, laugh.

I couldn't, even though I wanted to, stay mad.

Whatever she was saying was showing me how. What it was going to be like to be a woman.

She had her hands on my waist so I wouldn't fall off.

Daddy raised the camera. He was calling my name.

THE EQUATOR

My father walked me down the spiral staircase.

He held my hand, he was *nervous as a wreck*, he was crying.

I was his bride descending the stair. He held my hand, tears like petals in my hair.

In the Northern Hemisphere, water swirls counterclockwise.

Called it *a flaw in the ointment, a monkey in the wrench.*

Held me on his lap, named the birds, carried me into the endless ocean.

Junket, oriole, Der Rosenkavalier.

Made us all listen to the train through the living room, *stereophonic sound.*

Taught us good manners. *Don't talk with your mouth open. Never hand Daddy anything filled with a snake.*

Punched my mother in the stomach, *cardinal, chickadee.*

Held my hand, hosted parties for Ike.

Never saw a movie he hadn't seen before.

Held me up in the waves, *tanager, cedar waxwing*, pulled panicking a towel around his naked waist.

Slammed the bathroom door in my face. White space.

But blue tufted couch, blue smoke of his cigarette, *indigo bunting.*

Let me bury my face in his neck, *good-bye.*

Disappeared (again) overseas, into *Atlas Shrugged*, his second wife, into the gin that (HINTS FROM HELOISE) brings wilted lilacs back to life.

Signed himself: *Devotedly, Dad.*

In the Southern Hemisphere water spirals clockwise.

Then he sat in his easy chair by the library window. He smelled of red leather, martinis, Chesterfields.

I sat across from him on the couch in the middle of Saturday, woods at a distance repeating themselves, this used to be my house, this used to be my dad, there was nothing for us to say to each other.

Not one word. Not one bird.

Woods like an echo.

Nothing when I smoked, when I drank said nothing, but (once upon a time) had named the birds.

Equinox, equator, *in medias res.*

Day divided equally from night.

Humankind at the crack, the crack of.

Here water falls like grief, straight down.

TROPICS S

Hole in the map of the known world, burning between my feet.

I was like Will, I was crying. I was like Buddy, I was not.

Go back overseas, my mother said, *your father would have wanted.*

American cars so fat, obese the houses, highways, headstones.

Three days at home, violent, violet thunderstorms.

My mother's voice over the deep-sea cable.

Like colliding tectonic plates.

Your father's dead.

o

Then Freddie said he thought he was in love with me.

I loved Freddie, he was never a hundred percent sure.

o

My knees being weak. His whispering being all the old standards in my ear.

Nobody ever sang to me, nobody ever called me *baby* until Freddie.

o

Freddie thought *infinitesimal* meant infinite, only more so.

I'm your father, he accused me.

So what, I'm your mother.

o

Freddie said, *You're the most selfish person I ever met.*

Then he married me.

o

Penises so small, so ugly, *heart-rendering* (as my father used to say).

(Though not about penises).

Smell of a man's spent sex like lead pencil shavings.

o

In the blacked-out hotel room we woke that first morning facing each other in our tangled nest.

That face with arched brows, flushed cheeks, the good mouth.

Freddie opened his great brown eyes, he looked at me.

I looked at him looking at me looking.

No difference, no daylight between.

o

My mother once said there's *a point beyond which.*

As with temper or glare and would such a person ever come back.

One time I slapped Freddie full in the face.

Or passion. Who started it.

o

I came up out of a blackout, his hands around my neck, squeezing.

It feels that good.

o

I didn't marry you, said Freddie, *because you could cook.*

o

It wasn't the first time: *open marriage* like a book.

Open marriage like a wound.

Open marriage like a door.

o

Your brains is in your cocks and your cocks beeps like radar.

You pants like lap dogs wherever they wags: *Susie Sally Rita Pita.*

Plays footsies with Fifi. Fondles Harriet Iscariot.

Punches Prunella in her *a cappella.*

While Lucy goes liquid for you to drinks, you smiles all the whiles at Svetlana, that sluts.

Stay away from him, I tells her, *you blonde bitch.*

You don'ts own him, she yell back.

o

All maps being distortions.

A sphere being a sphere, irreducible to the flat white world of paper.

o

I was so drunk.

Diamonds dripping from my ears, between my breasts, blood between my legs. In the white gown, in the plush casino, words gushing up from who knows where, when he turned around in the glare.

Out of the minutes, out of the degrees.

I was so drunk, when he slapped I didn't cry, I didn't turn on my heel and walk.

o

I was so drunk. I felt the belt in my hand, his soft skin.

I wanted to beat him and beat and beat.

Him and my brothers and my mother and my father and would such a person ever come back.

The point beyond which. Beyond it.

o

I was so drunk, crouching above him, his mouth between my legs. He closed his eyes against the sting.

He opened his mouth as wide but he couldn't, not wide enough, I thought he was going to drown, but he didn't.

It ran down his cheeks and into his hair, around his neck onto the carpet, the towel I wished we had put underneath us, how would we ever get it out.

What will the housekeeper say when she sees it, what does she make of the sheets.

o

I was so drunk. His hands at my throat. I knew I had to come out of that blackout, or else.

o

There are no landmarks in this country.

o

Joined an archeological expedition. Got drunk every night, slept with a man who said *I dig bones.*

Bathed in a sulphur spring, smelled like hell. Stayed out all day naked in the desert sun.

Walked the hills, found nothing. Dug in the dirt, found nothing.

But rocks (I thought): Scotch on the, marriage on the.

o

Came home from three weeks in the semi-arid desert.

Turn off the TV, I told Freddie, I want to talk to you.

Drew crude maps of old fire pit dust. Sifted sides of mountains through a standing sieve. Painted little numbers on dozens of arrowheads. Learned to call them *points*.

I'm leaving.

o

Learned to recognize obsidian that was *worked*.

Surveyed mountains. Drank bad wine. Fell into beds, one of which was mine.

I'm leaving.

o

Watched a man kill a rattlesnake with a stick. Burned the skin all over my body. Ate bad mayonnaise left out overnight.

The little oblong pit in Freddie's freckled back.

I'm leaving.

o

Oh, the sharp living fragrance of sagebrush after rain.

Falling in love with the ugly scrub desert.

How Freddie rolled his shirtsleeves to the elbow.

I'm leaving.

THE INTEMPERATE ZONE

Hello, I dreamed, and nobody stared. Nobody laughed, though they all had their clothes on. Margo put her arm around my shoulders, *Hi hon*. She drew me behind the green counter. She called to one of the others, who brought a uniform; she helped me into the black and white checked dress with the pretty white starched collar and pretty white starched cuffs on the pretty white capped sleeves. She tied the apron in a white starched bow. She gave me a pair of white socks and black sneakers. They fit. Then she placed a headband on my black and white hair like a white starched crown. It read Happy New Year. She showed me the kitchen. She taught me *whiskey down*.

o

I make circles with my pencil (feather duster) in the air.

I don't know what to do with myself.

I haven't had a drink in two weeks.

o

It's all uphill from here, whispers my dead father in my ear.

o

Still, I thought everything would be changed.

The first time I stayed up past midnight, the first time I stayed up till dawn, the day I got married.

Ah, but my first drink.

o

Please, Freddie said when I tried to give up smoking, *please have a cigarette*.

o

Raise your arm, says Tolstoy.

You think it's free will but it's not. The whole chain of events from the start has led you up to.

Have a drink, said Freddie.

o

If the earth revolves around the sun, if *cogito ergo sum,* if reason reasons only with itself, if chance, if no plan, if whatever happens, that's what it means, if ruled by our subconsciouses, if time equals space, if the world is mostly interstices, if relative, if probably, if we can blow the world to *kingdom come,* if language grumbles to itself alone.

o

In short:

For my eighteenth birthday, I bought myself a cocktail dress.

Martinis rampant on a navy field, embroidered down the side the heart is on.

o

I put glow-in-the-dark tape on the ashtray I used when I smoked in bed.

I may be a drunk, I told Freddie, but I'm not stupid.

o

How I spun from the midnight curve of the piano past the treacherous fountain beneath the stairs, landed just where I prayed I would, leg flung up on the newel post, head back, chiffon trailing on the peacock-feather rug under my bare and toenail-painted pointed foot.

o

I could not keep my eyes open. In the middle of an incomprehensible sentence—the one I myself was speaking—one lid lowered almost completely, the other fallen to the middle of my eye, two yellow eyeballs rolling round like planets, capillaries fizzling out.

The number of bottles of red wine consumed was four amongst six people, three of whom weren't drinking.

Resting my head on the back of my chair, surveying our guests at an angle whereby I could just keep my nose above water.

But not my brain stem.

o

I need help, I said.

What you need is another drink, said my darling Freddie.

o

How liquid, what rapture of the deep.

Makes you believe you can breathe under water.

Sings in your ear: *Take off that tank, your phony mask of oxygen, put on a happy face.*

Now I know what I've got. This must be the bends.

o

The French don't die of arteriosclerosis. They drink red wine.

Like, how you say, zee roto rooter.

What the French do die of is liver failure.

Neverzeeless.

o

Today is my 22nd day without a drink.

Landscape, as in a cartoon, repeats itself.

This truth holds also for wallpaper.

o

Once upon a time, there was a pretty little girl in strawberry curls dressed in polished cotton pink and pinky bows and pampered.

Pearls like rope around her pretty neck.

Whiskers on her chin and whiskey on her breath.

Toss it back, mouth on sleeve, don't need nobody. One o' the boys.

o

I thought I needed more sunshine in the winter. I thought I was depressed.

The doctor recommended I sit every day underneath a *gro-light* for fifteen minutes.

I poured myself a drink. I abandoned my theory.

This may have had something to do with the word *gro*.

What you need is a good night's sleep, said Freddie.

o

March sun steals into frozen gardens, pale fingers on cold skin after too long absence, first slow anxiety of birth.

Makes me shiver.

Water seeps into roots, seeds turn green.

In the maple trees sap like memory begins to push along the veins, liquid feeling of fear these mornings.

I don't want to wake up to.

o

This pervasive, all-encompassing light, said one of my fellow alcoholics.

We were at a meeting.

My limbs were numb. I had to blink several times. It was very, very quiet. I lifted my arm up over my head to shade my eyes. It hurt to lift it.

I thought I was going to see, I wasn't sure, God maybe.

I'd passed out in the middle of the night with all the lights on, blazing.

o

What I needed the next morning was the sound of rice growing.

o

Excuse me, I told the hairdresser, I think my hair's uneven on one side.

He said, how can your hair be uneven on one side. He said he thought I must be drunk. He said, it's either even or it's not.

I said, you either get paid or you don't.

o

There was an incident involving this girl throwing a cupcake in my face when I was ten.

I came home in a depression that over the years I drank to get rid of.

Now I've stopped drinking, the cupcake is back.

o

I used to go out to walk the dog and forget the dog.

○

I was going on a date. My father didn't want me to.

We had a huge fight. I ran out of the house, yelling, Drop dead!

He came after me. He had a heart attack on the driveway.

My mother stood at the top of the stairs.

Now look what you've done, she said. You've killed your father.

○

Once upon a time I had a chipmunk. He liked to nestle in my neck. When I ate dinner, I set him a plate of nuts at the table. They puffed out his stomach and his cheeks.

He always slept with me at night. Sometimes he crawled into the hollow of my back, but I always pulled him out.

One night I came home drunk. I was very drunk. I was fairly drunk. I was totaled.

I fell asleep with my clothes on. The chipmunk must have crawled under the small of my back.

When I woke up the next morning, he was dead. Asphyxiated.

That was the day I knew.

I was never going to have another chipmunk.

o

My husband said he thought the spinach wasn't quite done.

When I looked I saw I'd served it to him straight from the freezer, a hard green brick.

That was the night I knew.

So I tried white wine.

So I tried divorce.

o

Cartographers have a choice, Harry says.

Either distort the size of a continent or change its shape.

o

Two bottles of Wild Turkey, a bottle of Teacher's, a bottle of Canadian Club one shot down, a bottle of Stolichnaya, a bottle of Gordon's Gin, half a bottle of Beefeater's for Peter, an unopened bottle of Ron Rico because nobody seems to drink rum anymore, a bottle of Grand Marnier, a bottle of Metaxa, a bottle of vin santo in memory of Aunt Phoebe, a bottle of saki Gloria gave me who loves sushi, two decanters, one full of Scotch, the other full of brandy, one a wedding present from Freddie's uncle, the other my mother's doughnut-shaped beauty, the last bottle of white wine, three bottles of red, a bottle of Harvey's Bristol Cream.

The sink smelled wonderful.

This is my 34th day without a drink.

o

This is my 34th day without a drink, say I.

There's a pause, an *uh*.

That's wonderful, says Judy.

I don't think I could do that, Gloria says.

You know, you look back over the last month and you try to think of one night when you didn't have a drink and there isn't one, says Peter.

I quit cold turkey a couple of times, says Frank, *but within a couple of months I was saying, oh, I can have a Scotch now and then, and I was back.*

o

I'm not an alcoholic, I don't drink before sundown.

I don't get hung over.

I only drink rosé.

I've never been arrested.

I sleep in Grand Central Station. If I was an alcoholic, I'd be sleeping in the Port Authority.

I ain't dead yet.

o

These, my friends, are the widest latitudes.

o

One day I couldn't find the baby's pacifier. When bedtime came I still hadn't found it. I told him I was afraid it was gone, rolled up in the dirty bed sheets, sent to the Chinese laundry. For good. I kissed him goodnight and hugged him, thinking he'd never be able to sleep.

But he did, he fell asleep. He woke up. He ate, he played, he slept again. I don't get it.

o

Remote areas of New Guinea, for instance, still marked *No Data Available.*

o

Maybe he won't turn out to be an alcoholic. Maybe he's not like me.

o

I used to see Albert in the neighborhood when he was still walking with a cane.

We talked. I thought I was a light unto his darkness.

He called me several times for lunch.

I hated being seen with him, I hated the thought that people might think we were together.

He shook, his clothes were torn, his hair was dirty, stubble in odd patches grew on his cheeks and throat.

I asked him please to stop telling me he loved me.

How are *you*, I asked, after running out of things to say about myself.

This is life, he shrugged, *it goes on*.

o

Yesterday Albert showed up at Soup Kitchen in the golf cart he uses now for a wheelchair.

We talked. His hand and arm were shaking very badly.

How are *you*, I asked. *This is life, it goes on*.

o

I was slicing carrots when the phone rang.

Albert said he'd been in love with me for fifteen years.

He said he'd back off but would I have lunch.

I said sure. He warned me I'll be having lunch with a man who is madly in love with me.

o

An azimuthal projection, says Harry, *places one particular point at the center of the map, which is observed from the zenith directly above that point.*

It's my alcoholism, it's my solipsism, it's my alcoholism, it's my solipsism, alcy, soly, alcy, soly, sism sism sism.

o

What you need is a good fuck, said Freddie.

o

Freddie said he was a *functioning* alcoholic.

By this he meant not in spite of, but because.

This is my 65th day without a drink.

o

Ivy on the brick wall, rust red flaring into licks of flame.

Evening sun like a coat of feathers the wind lifts.

Flowers blooming, or not (quite) (yet).

Water about to spill over and over.

I love that.

o

I'm fighting with a stranger, beautiful hair of blue.

Trying to wrestle a beer can from me, a beer can I think is me.

I'm clutching it to my breast.

The angel has his foot in the small of my back, bending.

o

Today is my 90th day.

And what comes after 90? somebody asks.

Everybody answers, *Ninety-one.*

ANTARCTIC CONVERGENCE

So I was saying how my mother's ashes flew up in our faces.

My wedding ring flew from my finger across the counter, I heard it *ping*.

Following a perfect parabola of light, I found it resting at a stranger's feet.

Behind him through the window a tall sky tinged his light hair blue.

You have to appreciate, he drawled, *the grand gesture.*

Ladies and gents, meet Lionel.

o

A southern continent was projected by the ancient geographer Ptolemy.

For reasons, says Harry, *of aesthetic balance.*

o

Sam sticks his snout in, he sniffs and sniffs. Powder on his whiskers, fur of his snout, white eyelashes.

I can almost sense, almost remember.

Ice deep in the nostrils, cold ancient knowledge of the lungs.

Then I just want to keep opening in.

o

We tried a turtle. We tried a gerbil. One day we wandered, Harry and I, into a pet store.

Sam was lying on his back in a traveling case, all four legs splayed apart, tongue directly under the water bottle spout.

White and round as a dandelion.

Two weeks from now, I said. If you still want him. If he's still there.

o

Sam and I walked Harry all the way to school each morning and back again every afternoon.

Orange and red hemline of sky at the ends of the streets looking east, looking west.

o

He pees on a stack of *Yellow Pages* left at the curb.

Dog wit, dog etiquette.

o

The vet says it's just a matter of nursing, how long can we last.

o

Sam didn't eat this morning, he was sick all night.

I asked the vet about sleeping pills.

What did he say, Harry asked.

He said Thorazine, he said Valium.

Well, maybe it would be okay as long as Sam doesn't horde them, said Lionel.

o

You have to remember Sam was a puppy when I was still drinking.

o

I'll scatter his ashes across the Drake Passage or onto the ice on a white midnight.

I'll buy a pretty perfume bottle to put his ashes in.

Opaque, Lionel specifies.

o

He lays back his ears in the redolent wind.

What is the body's knowledge, that it can tell how soon, how close the snow is coming.

Each breath flying to stitch a tear that cannot mend.

Dazzling, how the light pours in.

o

He died in my lap.

I leaned down to kiss him good-bye, Harry said, *Behave yourself.*

Lionel licked my tears.

o

Aren't the crocuses pretty, said Lionel.

They remind me of Sam.

You mean because we went over there to look at them with him, asked Harry.

Because now that he can come back in any shape he wants, I thought he might come back as a crocus.

I have a feeling he'd come back as something more aggressive than a crocus, Lionel said.

Something white, though, said Harry.

o

He'll come back as Hamlet's father's ghost.

He'll come back as the whitest white stallion. Mother's milk.

Sam won't come back, the moon won't let him.

Egret. Bald eagle. White owl. Albatross.

Ice crystals suddenly forming in air.

Earth's axis. Stubborn white turtle the universe rests upon.

Sam will come back as black stones in a clear stream.

Sam will come back as the fire and ice. Messenger, Pegasus-winged.

Legs the pillars of Hercules. Eyes the sky's black sockets. White noise.

Tail curling over the back of the sky.

Good God, woman, he was only a dog, said Lionel.

o

How every absence implies a presence, each death a turbulent, hot and cold convergence.

Where, according to Harry, warm Atlantic waters meet Southern Ocean cold.

How every loss includes them all.

85

Besides, so what if he was only a dog, said Harry. *He was our dog.*

o

Don't want the ashes weighing any weight at all.

No *thing* to them, yet they are so like, having the heavy *ness* of matter.

As if, like a hole being burned in a map.

Through which the pain, the absence, the glare.

Or as if through a cloth, a tear. So that the thing is there, but not there.

o

Cellophane wrapping, purple ribbon, yellow fuzzy flower. Card reading:

The deceased has been individually cared for.

I may be sentimental, I told the vet, but I'm not stupid.

o

Two cups. Nevertheless. I carried him home in both arms.

o

Used to eat hose water.

Brought rocks home like bones.

Glass shatters on the street, no warning, no aftermath.

Leash no longer needed. He comes when we call.

All right, so I am stupid.

o

Where am I going to be buried now.

Either my ashes will merge with my mother's and sift through the lives of the people I love.

Or what's protocol for: with *his* family?

Or lying with my father, that passionate wish.

Daddy, this is Lionel.

o

The line moves with you. You can pull the white blankets over your head but you can't be together with the lost.

You fall back. Into the daylight, the meadow, the degrees.

Teeming with color, the thousand birds singing their welcome, blue sky, the infinite black recession of the stars.

Absence like a metaphor, sounds a Sam can hear.

Where the severed fingers go.

As if we'd fallen through, stuck a hand into the glare.

o

Then I'm alone, the wind blows cold across the open deck.

I turn the bottle upside down.

Petals of ash swirl into the air, onto the backs of the goony birds flying, onto the backs of the black ocean waves, leopard seals, chinstrap penguins, onto the icefloes, onto the islands.

Onto my white hair.

Like fresh snow. Ash snow.

o

Welcome home, says Lionel. He calls me *sweetheart*.

The sound of dishes being put back in the cupboard, even when I'm the one doing the putting.

I love that.

Tulips strewn across a double bed.

o

Lionel, you remind me of my second husband.

But I thought you'd only been married once.

Exactly.

THE SOUTH POLE

Glory in the highest, farthest, windiest, coldest, driest.

Continent so white, so pure, so locked away, maps of it read like blanks.

Like entering an atmosphere, an alternate, an after-life.

Beyond the whirlpool, inside (at last) the glare.

So, then, you're drawn to cold places, someone says.

Not necessarily, say I. I'm drawn to extremes.

From space, a planet slightly pear-shaped, flattened by its heavy metaphysics of polar ice.

From which weather systems, sea levels, ocean currents, breath.

Ice core traces of Krakatoa, Chernobyl, Pompeii, Hiroshima.

Barometer of whatever befalls.

And the ice grows like a living thing, crystal by crystal, cell by cell.

Takes on a life of its own, a kind of parody.

And I am an obstacle in the path of the wind. That is my only (funny) function in this place.

Though the mind (how improbable) will mediate, will speak.

Every hour a summer's day of daylight.

Every hour a winter's night of night.

Horizon crooning like love, *I'll never end.*

For desire must be made to thicken into meaning.

So we have reached, at last, the starting point.

Here the auroral fire, the breath-taking, breath-making diamond dust.

The ice moves outward, bearing the dead.

Air so clear you can hear them speaking.

World so white you can see them writing.

Home is everywhere. Home is nowhere. YOU ARE HERE.

Acknowledgments

An earlier version of "The Intemperate Zone" was published in *Deadsnake Apotheosis*.

Versions of "The North Pole," "Tropics N," and "Tropics S" are available at www.friggmagazine.com.

An earlier version of "The Equator" appeared in *xconnect*.

I am indebted throughout to Peter Whitfield, whose books about cartography have been a fascinating and entertaining resource, and to Stephen Pine, especially in "The South Pole," for his book *The Ice*.

Thanks to the Atlantic Center for the Arts, where this book was conceived.

Thanks to Harris Manchester College, Oxford University, which supported the writing.

Thanks to family, friends and colleagues who watched and helped the poem take shape along the way, especially Carolyn, Jason, and (most of all, every day) Leonard.

Laurel Blossom is the author of *Wednesday: New and Selected Poems* (Ridgeway Press, 2004). Earlier books include *The Papers Said* (Greenhouse Review Press, 1993), *What's Wrong* (Cobham & Hatherton Press, 1987), and *Any Minute* (Greenhouse Review Press, 1979). Her work has appeared in a number of anthologies, including *180 More: Extraordinary Poems for Every Day*, edited by Billy Collins (Random House, 2005), and in journals including *American Poetry Review, The Carolina Quarterly, Deadsnake Apotheosis, Harper's, Many Mountains Moving, The Paris Review, Pequod, Poetry*, and *Seneca Review*, among others. Blossom is the editor of *Splash! Great Writing about Swimming* (Ecco Press, 1996) and *Many Lights in Many Windows: Twenty Years of Great Fiction and Poetry from The Writers Community* (Milkweed Editions, 1997). She serves on the editorial board of *Heliotrope: a journal of poetry*. Blossom has received fellowships from the National Endowment for the Arts, the New York Foundation for the Arts, the Ohio Arts Council, and Harris Manchester College (Oxford University), where she serves on the Board of Regents. She co-founded the esteemed writing residency and workshop program The Writers Community. She serves on the boards of the Laura (Riding) Jackson Foundation in Vero Beach, Florida, and Edgefield Regional Arts in South Carolina. Blossom belongs to the Explorers Club and the Circumnavigators Club in New York City. She lives in rural South Carolina.